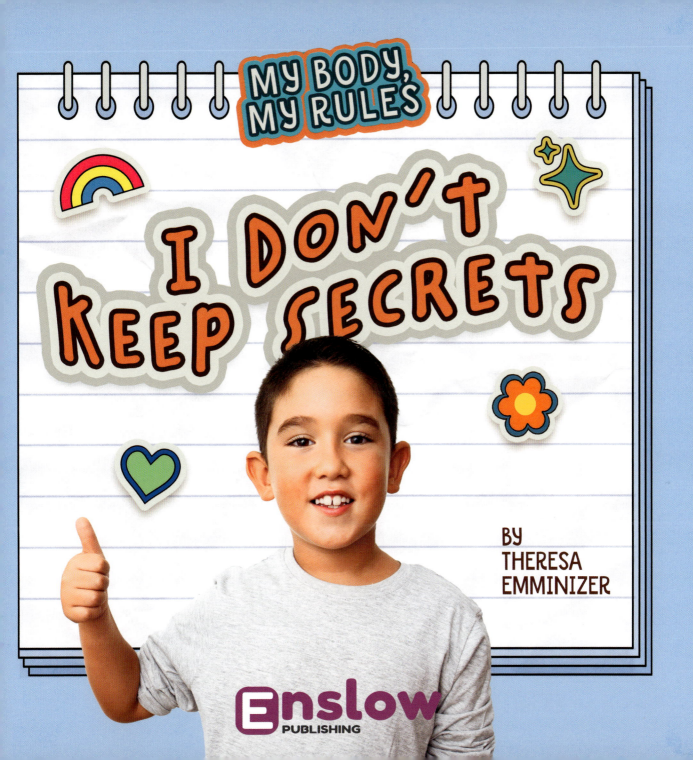

My Body, My Rules

I Don't Keep Secrets

By Theresa Emminizer

Enslow Publishing

Please visit our website, www.enslow.com.
For a free color catalog of all our high-quality books, call toll free 1-800-398-2504 or fax 1-877-980-4454.

Library of Congress Cataloging-in-Publication Data

Names: Emminizer, Theresa, author.
Title: I don't keep secrets / Theresa Emminizer.
Description: [Buffalo] : Enslow Publishing, [2025] | Series: My body, my rules | Includes bibliographical references and index. | Audience: Grades K-1
Identifiers: LCCN 2023053902 (print) | LCCN 2023053903 (ebook) | ISBN 9781978539389 (library binding) | ISBN 9781978539372 (paperback) | ISBN 9781978539396 (ebook)
Subjects: LCSH: Honesty–Juvenile literature. | Secrecy–Juvenile literature. | Conduct of life–Juvenile literature.
Classification: LCC BF723.H7 E46 2025 (print) | LCC BF723.H7 (ebook) | DDC 179/.9–dc23/eng/20231220
LC record available at https://lccn.loc.gov/2023053902
LC ebook record available at https://lccn.loc.gov/2023053903

Published in 2025 by
Enslow Publishing
2544 Clinton Street
Buffalo, NY 14224

Copyright © 2025 Enslow Publishing

Designer: Tanya Dellaccio Keeney
Editor: Theresa Emminizer

Photo credits: Series art (notebook) Design PRESENT/Shutterstock.com; series art (stickers) tmn art/Shutterstock.com; cover (boy) Krakenimages.com/Shutterstock.com; p. 5 stockfour/Shutterstock.com; p. 7 LightField Studios/Shutterstock.com; pp. 9, 11 fizkes/Shutterstock.com; pp. 13, 21 Monkey Business Images/Shutterstock.com; p. 15 Anna Kuzmenko/Shutterstock.com; p. 17 wavebreakmedia/Shutterstock.com; p. 19 Zulfiska/Shutterstock.com.

All rights reserved.
No part of this book may be reproduced in any form without permission in writing from the publisher, except by a reviewer.

Printed in the United States of America

Some of the images in this book illustrate individuals who are models. The depictions do not imply actual situations or events.

CPSIA compliance information: Batch #CSENS25: For further information contact Enslow Publishing, at 1-800-398-2504.

CONTENTS

WHAT'S A SECRET? 4
SECRETS HURT US 6
YOUR SAFETY CIRCLE 10
SECRETS AREN'T KIND 12
SECRETS AREN'T SAFE 14
SPOT UNSAFE SECRETS 16
NO SECRETS, JUST SURPRISES 18
WHAT TO DO 20
WORDS TO KNOW 22
FOR MORE INFORMATION 23
INDEX 24

BOLDFACE WORDS APPEAR IN WORDS TO KNOW.

What's a Secret?

A secret is something you hide from others. Secrets can make you feel bad, sad, or lonely. A friend or person you know might ask you to keep a secret. If that happens, say: "I don't keep secrets!"

SECRETS HURT US

Brooke was riding the school bus. An older boy sat down next to her. He showed Brooke a picture on his phone. The picture made Brooke feel **uncomfortable**. But the boy said: "You can't tell anybody. Or else!"

Brooke felt bad inside. Like she had done something wrong. Brooke was scared to tell her mom. Would her mom be mad? Would Brooke be in trouble? Brooke decided to tell her mom. Just saying it out loud made Brooke feel better.

TALKING TO HER MOM HELPED BROOKE FEEL SAFE AGAIN.

YOUR SAFETY CIRCLE

When something scary happens, it helps to talk to a safe grown-up. A safety circle is a group of adults you can trust. The people in your safety circle will always listen to you and believe you. You can tell them anything.

WHO'S IN YOUR SAFETY CIRCLE? THINK OF THREE SAFE ADULTS.

SECRETS AREN'T KIND

Annie was playing with her friends Tasha and Julie. Tasha and Julie were whispering to each other. Annie felt left out. She worried they were whispering about her. It hurt Annie's feelings that Tasha and Julie told secrets.

SECRETS CAN MAKE PEOPLE FEEL LEFT OUT.

SECRETS AREN'T SAFE

Sharing a secret with someone might make you feel close to them. It can feel good to be trusted. But secrets aren't just unkind, they're unsafe. Keeping a secret can put you or someone else in danger.

PROTECT YOURSELF AND OTHERS. DON'T KEEP SECRETS.

SPOT UNSAFE SECRETS

Spot unsafe secrets by asking these questions:

- Does this make me feel uncomfortable?
- Is it something mean about someone?
- Is someone being **harmed**?
- Is a rule being broken?
- Are we trying to cover something up?

NO SECRETS, JUST SURPRISES

Surprises are different from secrets. A surprise is something that will be told soon. Maybe it's a gift that you keep hidden but then give to your friend on their birthday. Unlike secrets, surprises feel good. Surprises make people happy!

WHAT TO DO

Secrets are hurtful, unkind, and unsafe. But if someone tells you to keep a secret, don't be scared! It's not your **fault**. You won't be in trouble. Share the truth with a safe adult. They'll help you make a plan to stay safe.

Words to Know

fault: A mistake or something done wrong.

harm: Hurt.

honesty: Truthfulness.

protect: To keep safe.

uncomfortable: Feeling unhappy or unsure about something.

FOR MORE INFORMATION

BOOKS

Ridley, Sarah. *Being Safe*. New York, NY: PowerKids Press, 2023.

Woolley, Katie. *Keeping Safe*. New York, NY: PowerKids Press, 2024.

WEBSITES

Fun Kids
www.funkidslive.com/learn/top-10-facts/top-10-facts-about-internet-safety/
Read these tips for staying safe online.

Kids Health
kidshealth.org/en/kids/handle-abuse.html
Learn what to do if someone is harming you.

Publisher's note to educators and parents: Our editors have carefully reviewed these websites to ensure that they are suitable for students. Many websites change frequently, however, and we cannot guarantee that a site's future contents will continue to meet our high standards of quality and educational value. Be advised that students should be closely supervised whenever they access the internet.

23

INDEX

feeling left out, 12, 13
feeling safe, 9, 10, 11, 17, 20, 21
feeling scared, 7, 8, 20
feeling uncomfortable, 6, 16
friends, 4, 5, 12
harm, 16
honesty, 21

rules, 16
safe adults, 8, 9, 10, 11, 17, 20
safety circle, 10, 11
spotting unsafe secrets, 16
surprises, 18, 19
trust, 10, 14
truth, 17, 20